The

I0448008

Streets

Have Eyes

A Harm City Book

Dust Cover

It has been said that the worst of times bring out the best in people and that the best of times brings out the worst in our kind. *The Streets Have Eyes* offers both views from the gutters, bus stops, alleys and public latrines of Baltimore Maryland.

This is a book about characters, from the outrageously defiant and the interestingly adrift, to the disgusting and the morbidly debased. *The Streets Have Eyes* is a tale of postmodern urban anti-wonder.

The Streets Have Eyes is intended as a pocket color commentary companion to the daring tourists who the author plans on leading in Harm City Safari Tours. Keep it at hand so you might be the first to spot an infamous denizen of the ghetto. Just remember to keep your window closed and do not feed the locals!

The Streets Have Eyes

Contents

For Stick, I hope you found your way

"Every town is different
Every face will change"

-Ursula Ricks, **Tobacco Road**, from the album **My Street**

Preface

A round about 2006 I no longer regarded Harm City as a hazard to be survived but rather as a curiosity—for it can never rise to the structure of a wonder in my mind's eye—to be studied. This might have to do with the fact that I had become a management person in my line of toil and was beginning to organize meets in the fighting world. Whether one stage builds on the other or rather rejects the previous, I do not know.

Where prior to this time I looked upon every person as an enemy and delved into the mechanics of their perspective demise at my ready hands, I now viewed the world of street people as an anthropological preserve. Rather than glaring I was merely reticent or on occasion engaging. I had become a student of the culture of decay where previously I had been a student of its violent expression.

Eventually, as a coaching fighter I was called on to relate encounters of the violent kind, and becoming bored with the line of my own inquiry, would veer off into recounting encounters of the vile kind, if for no other reason than to lighten the mood. I was becoming a story teller. So apparently I can thank Harm City for more than providing a laboratory for aggression, but a backdrop for expression as well.

Offhand I cannot recall most of the tales that I am about to copy off of my website and post in the space below. I will wager though, that little violence will occur in the pages of this book, for it is a haphazard record of my observations of this deteriorating ecosystem's more colorful inhabitants.

If you were expecting the urban equivalent of big game hunting tales you are about to be disappointed, for if surviving the lethal intentions of street thugs can be equated to big game hunting, then this book amounts to bird watching. Even if disappointed I wager you shall be entertained.

James LaFond, Wednesday 10/15/2014

The Streets Have Eyes #1: From Hood-rats to Heavy Metal Meat-munchers

© 2013 James LaFond

The Vigilante Conundrum of the Crack Epidemic

The 1990s in Baltimore was a watershed of violent crime. During this period I hit bottom, and became what I would now describe as a borderline psychopath. The tipping point for me had nothing to do with being threatened every week, attacked every month, or even shot at, during my commutes to and from work as a pedestrian and bus patron. I found all of that to be rather interesting.

The two things that pushed me over the edge were my wife and children being threatened and attacked; and me being repeatedly stalked. The anger of having my helpless family members threatened when I wasn't there was the tinder. The actual experience of having criminals hunt me on foot, and with automobiles, was the spark that turned me into a whack job. The fact that I could not outrun vehicles or teenage hood-rats set me to breaking the law in order to protect myself.

10

During that period I walked the streets of Baltimore with illegal firearms, and combat blades, up to and including swords. My life became a game of 'are the cops going to be hassling me tonight' or are 'the hood-rats going to be ambushing me?' I usually made the right call and went out unarmed when the cops were looking for me and armed when the criminals were looking for me. Eventually it became too much stress and I decided to cache improvised weapons along my regular routes, at bus-stops, and in various desolate locales where I would lead those punks who followed me through side-streets and alleys and parks after I got off the bus.

Now, having turned Baltimore's decaying structures and overgrown byways into my arsenal, I just lost it; and left the house every night resigned to a violent death and the bleak hope to take someone with me. A lot of the results have found their way into my various survival books and articles. But there were also the strange and weird encounters that my courting of danger engendered. Some have been interspersed through my first book as comic relief, and some tales have never been told. So I conceived of this look into the 1990s underbelly of Baltimore, as experienced by an oddball urban survivalist walking the edge of sanity.

At the time I was a thin long-haired loner, clean shaven, and sporting a bandana with either American Indian or Confederate motifs, depending on who I wanted to antagonize. The street people often mistook me for a Lumbee Indian. My street names when clean shaven were Rambo, Tarzan, Cain and Tonto; when bearded in winter Caveboy was what they called me the most. During the period when I began accepting lifts from anybody that pulled over, I had stopped carrying combat knives. If armed I usually settled for a hammer, screwdriver, or some kind of razor or ink pen.

Earl's Crew

Eighteen years ago a crew of teenage drug-dealers were using my oldest son to hold their pager. They had threatened him, robbed him, attacked him, and then kept him quiet by threatening to hurt his mother. We could not even keep a winter coat on his back. One of his friends filled me in and I tracked Earl, the set leader, down. His four boys came after me at a bus stop one night and lost their nerve. They retaliated by calling my wife and telling her that they had killed me. I went insane and called Earl at his mother's house, to give a detailed description of the fate he had just earned. He was a tall 17-year-old who walked around in a Malcolm X outfit, and bipedal locomotion was a privilege he had just forfeited. I thought he should be aware of his upcoming handicapped status.

His forty-something mother interceded with violent threats against my family; the 'queen pin' of their drug network I suppose. I told her, "If those four boys in the BMW are the best you can do"...and then I descended into a rant about killing her son, torturing and binding her, raping her daughter, eating her dog, and roasting her small children over the bonfire that had been her house. I had become a psychopath when backed against that wall at the back of the starkest part of my mind. One more threat from Earl or his crew and I would head down the street with a gas can and a machete.

My parents had grown up in the idyllic 1950s, and had imbued me with their ethics, as evidenced by my willingness to settle down and raise a family. I now knew from hard experience that their peace-and-love wait-for-the-cops-to-show-up mindset was not compatible with the reality that I faced. At this point in my ghettoized Fort Apache of a life I

13

had finally cast aside all of the reasons they had instilled in me for coexisting with an evil world. If I could not at least protect my family, I would take an equal number of the enemy off of the planet as a preemptive strike. I would not go to work leaving my dependents defenseless in a city with a [then] 45-minute police response time for a home invasion in progress. [This is now 10-15 minutes in Baltimore.] I decided that the very next threat from a member of that drug gang was my tripwire—the end of my life.

After that incident the young men in the area all avoided me. Earl was killed in the projects. One of the others was capped down the street. The evil mother moved. I should have rejoiced in their fate, but could not. I was still left with that hole in my soul that I had ripped open that day, when I had committed myself to the vilest acts imaginable. I decided against trying to patch it up, and settled on a slow interesting suicide; letting the sick world filter through it in hopes that enough debris would get caught in the self-installed psychological orifice to effect a plug. I had no end game, and hardly realized at the time that I was beginning my journey as a real writer; not just a scribbling fantasist or history buff.

I immediately began accepting all solicitations: punks that threatened me on the nocturnal bus stop encountered a nut-job that just wanted to die killing them; panhandlers encountered a Mister Hide like animal; dope-fiends, whack-jobs and sexual predators cruising around as illegal cabbies always got a $10 from me as I hopped into their ride and palmed my razor, wondering if this was the end. It was a dark time and has found expression in non-fiction form as When You're Food, and in some of my fiction as well. I will tell the most interesting tales spawned by this 'letting go of my social senses' in this series of articles. The first one is the story below, which also shows up in a piece I did on 'show wrestling.'

The Heavy Metal Meat-munchers

I was waiting for a bus at 9:45 on a Saturday night when a guy speeding down Route #1 in a black Toyota pickup skidded, slammed it into reverse, and zipped back to me, running his rear wheel up onto the curb, and yelled out the window, "Hey dude, where you goin?"

I said, "To East Point, to the supermarket."

He yelled, "When do you have to be there?"

I answered, "Eleven."

He whooped, "Then get in man! The Heavy Metal Marauder is breaking bad tonight."

I then got in the vehicle of a self-described superhero who was dressed all in black and was wearing a black knit hat in June and somehow forget to tell my wife about it the next day.

The man's name was Nelson, and he was in his mid-twenties, living in his deceased parents' house, still obsessed with a high school sweetheart that had become a Playboy Bunny, was waging a guerilla war on the local rock radio station on behalf of some 'underground heavy metal station', and fancied himself a pro wrestler.

Nelson drove aimlessly around telling me his life story and of the waging of the Metal versus Rock war, and assuring me that I would be to work on time. He remembered how important a job could be. After all he had had one once upon a time. Nelson did talk in the third person, which is always a red flag. What really got me worried was that, instead of raising his voice like a pro wrestler to stress a statement, he drew an explanation mark in the air with his finger.

Eventually we pulled up to a large seemingly abandoned frame house in Rosedale, a working class enclave on the city/county line on the East Side. It was early summer and the grass had yet to be cut. The shrubs had not been trimmed in years. He crashed through a makeshift backdoor and welcomed me to his castle, or should I say lair.

Nelson then began knocking back vodka and showing me the posters of his former girlfriend which she had even autographed—before she ran screaming for her life I suppose. Nelson showed me all the holes he had punched and kicked in the walls practicing Heavy Metal Combat, and then introduced me to a vast living room with a boarded up bay window. The floor was covered in old mattresses and he dove into the air, landing with a roll, and then demonstrated an elbow drop. Then he lay on his side and asked me if I wanted to wrestle. He was about 6 foot 200 lbs, in an altered state, and I was 5' 8" and an emaciated 147 lbs and still clinging to my tenuous sanity.

Run! I thought.

But I had my dignity to consider. What would Robert E. Howard's ghost think if I ran?

I excused myself to go to the bathroom—meaning all the while to flee for my life. I had, like a witless German peasant in a Grimm's fairy tale, been disoriented by the heaped trash and broken furniture, and lost my way. I got to a door at the end of a dark hallway and was then frightened more fully when a snarling, slathering, snapping of jaws and the clawing of nails and the crashing of heavy bodies sounded on the other side of the now trembling door.

Nelson's hand then came to rest on my shoulder and he said calmly, "You don't want to go in there. That's the Heavy Metal Meat-munchers; Rotts."

I remember thinking to myself, *Oh yeah, they are the big muscular Dobermans with pit-bull heads...and there are no large bags of dog-food in sight—priority egress!*

I put up a manly front though, "Thanks Nelson, I need to piss man."

He walked me away from the Door of Doom, "The plumbing is shot. Let's use the yard and then go on a mission..."

Yes, a mission! Why had I not thought of that reasonable alternative to psychotic mattress wrestling and a brief gory end as dog chow?

After doing a 'raid' on a local billboard by plastering his underground radio stickers on it as I fidgeted nervously in the cab of the Toyota among his promotional supplies, which—yes, I'm glad you asked—did include duct tape, he finally dropped me off in front of the store. Nelson gave me his phone number in case I ever needed a lift or just wanted to wrestle. I thanked him and donated some gas money to the 'war effort' and got out.

Big Rich, the night captain, was out front waiting for me and just looked on in amazement as Nelson finally cranked up the radio station he was so supportive of and drove off with eyes wild with excitement. Rich, who is incapable of communicating below a shout, of course shouted, "Christ Mo, smoke crack much!?!"

There was one time, years later, when I was fleeing from an ex girlfriend who was trying to run me over, that I finally got desperate enough to pull out the business card I had written Nelson's number on. I figured if anyone would be up for an emergency it would be him. But lo and behold, I had, at some point, sweated through the wallet and the ink on the card had bled...

Immunity to Gravity: Some Thoughts on Junky Superpowers

© 2013 James LaFond

I know that some of my readers are superhero movie and comic fans. So, when I was on the 10:00 PM bus this past Friday night a dim light went off in the back of my dark mind. You see, the ghetto has long hid its very own type of superhero; not a leading man with the cape; and not exactly an evil eccentrically dressed mastermind. Rather, this vile denizen of the ruined cities is more akin to a dark ally of either. Not necessarily aligned with good or evil, he or she never-the-less possesses rarified superpowers due to his exposure to a toxic substance...

For the everyday Harm Cityite substance abuse in general provides fear, loathing—and entertainment! Some examples follow from between the dust-coated cover of my tome of sage tales and arcane lore.

I and an entire busload of people once watched a crack-head attempt to walk up a light-pole on Charles Street. You see crack-heads have a difficult time controlling their superpowers, and he was unable to harness the gravity defying secrets sought by his kind. He was entertaining however, and sometimes managed to take a second step up the pole in his worn sneakers—which had lost their ability to squeak—before his foot would slide back down the pole and slingshot his face into the pavement...

Alcohol is a more reliable element for harnessing one's superhero powers, particularly when it becomes time to fight the cops! The stories of such applications of the power of alcohol are legion. So, instead of the predictable 'brains in a bottle' violence tale, I will regale you with a tale of alcohol used to harness the astral powers of The Universe to see into past lives and understand...

Ponca

I was once headed into town down Eastern Avenue after an argument with my scum-bag boss who would not pay me for my overtime [I think, although I am hazy on this twenty years gone.]. I got off at my normal transfer point at Ponca, beneath the hospital, in the bowels of Greek Town, where methadone clinic people would trade their methadone to street dealers for heroin. This is a major hub, servicing four bus lines, right at an interstate ramp. It was a Saturday morning.

A black couple was under the shelter in the gathering rain. A homeless woman who looked like Whoopie Goldberg with mange was yelling at two white trash guys who would not give her money or cigarettes, or whatever she was begging for. I remember her calling them racists. She also panhandled the black couple and was rejected.

She then went over to a trash can, took a swig from a large liquor bottle, belched with lawnmower-like authority, and came over to me. She put her arm around me, encased as it was in a garment that might have been a rug, a tapestry, or an ancient sweater, and yelled across the street to them, "That's alright, I don't need ya'all, 'cause I've got my friend here."

I remember thinking to myself, "Wow, what does that make me?"

At this time I was clean shaven and long haired and wore a bandana, and was often mistaken by street people as a Lumbee Indian, which are half-white to begin with. 'Ponca', however, assured me that I was a Navaho, or had been in a past life, and that she had long been a friend of members of my nation. She then—and remarkably she did not stink of anything worse than alcohol—began telling me about her connections with my ancestors. I recall her saying something about being close 'to your people'. I specifically remember her saying, "I have good friends who are members of the Navaho Nation."

Other than that all I can gather from the past is that she believed that we had a mystical connection, a connection I was but dimly aware of in my unaltered state.

She took a break and relieved herself of much liquid from a very aborigine squat in the middle of the median as motorists whizzed by. I took this opportunity to try and lose her under the shelter. She followed, and kept following me around, convinced of our otherworldly connection, her astral memory piqued by her magical nectar. The young lady under the stop hugged her man and smiled up at me, "Awwe, she likes you!"

After some time the black dude looked up at me— new to the Eastside as I was—"Hey man, you waiting on the twenty-two?"

"Yeah."

He smiled, "Well, the twenty-two don't come this far on the weekends. You'll be waiting here with this crazy bitch until Monday morning."

I thanked him, said goodbye to my soothsaying weird woman, and walked off into the rain, afraid of her magic...

The alcoholics are a mixed batch, ranging from those who use the magic to harness warrior spirits to fight 'The Man' and those few like Ponca who gazed into the firmament of The Universe. But, more often than not, it is just a brief comic relief for a busload of bored people, as the poor sot stumbles off the bus and is unable to apply the brakes as they career headfirst into a trashcan. Heroin addicts, however, have that under control, or should I say it has them...

Rat Face

Two nights ago, the bus stopped as soon as I boarded and took my seat. The driver was admitting a figure of elder repose, a hermit like creature of medieval proportions hunched under a burden, like the old peasant on the front of Led Zeppelin's Stairway to Heaven album. As the being stumbled past the meter we saw that it was male, with a wind-burned face, appearing perhaps 40. The puffy coat was torn and stained. He labored under a bag of trash and a baby stroller, without the baby. He tried to sit next to a young woman, who he called 'sweetie', in a voice barely 25-years-old, as he leaned into her in a hovering magnetic way, apparently defying gravity. She fled.

For ten minutes, on the rocking bus, he bent and twisted and held his head nearly to his ankle, cocking his ear like a squirrel that has heard a cat, as he reached, and groped, and finally found his bus ticket. By the time he had swiped the ticket the front bench seat was covered with the contents of his pockets, including many gutter-scrounged cigarettes.

I and two ladies remained up front. For the next five minutes he rocked and swayed, nearly standing on his head. The people in the back of the bus were beginning to enjoy the show, particularly the cringing of the two ladies who wrinkled their noses in fear and disgust at the thought of him falling onto them. They, neophyte Harm Cityites, did not yet realize that he had Immunity to Gravity!

The bus driver told him to sit, so he did, kind of parallel to the floor, with a hip and an elbow touching the triple bench seat, drool yo-yoing toward the floor, and arms and legs everywhere. The ladies were convinced that he would fall at any moment. People in the back were taking bets as to which one he would fall on. He never fell. This creature all but levitated above the seats. When it finally appeared that he would fall he would spring up on one foot, mumble an incantation, and begin weaving in the aisle, head between his knees, one hand up to God, and the other one trying to rub the spot from his pants that was not there.

Eventually I offloaded, reminding him to bring his stroller, and at least make an attempt to find the missing baby. The older woman, gasped at the possibility of a weekend custody disaster gone wrong and I wished the driver goodnight. As I crossed the street the driver stopped the bus in mid intersection as the gravity defying acrobat scrambled down from the bus with his baby carriage and attempted to follow me, as if I were someone that needed to be followed to some sacred place. As I outpaced him, my thoughts drifted to Ponca—or were they drawn forth through the void?

Was Ponca out there somewhere, pissing on a median strip, knocking back liquor, wondering if her gravity defying familiar had tracked down her old Navaho friend yet?

I scratched my beard and went on my way, wondering where the baby that belonged in that new, clean, carriage was.

The Streets Have Eyes #2: Bruce the Bricklayer

© 2013 James LaFond

A Summery Saturday Night, circa 1994

I was nearly to my bus stop on Belair Road, had just rounded the corner off of Southern Avenue, when I heard the rumble of a big pickup truck. A chill went up my spine as I heard the rattling thunder of the vehicle most favored by runt-stompers. I, being a runt, looked over my shoulder to see if I had time to run into the car lot. I noticed immediately that something was wrong: three fat bodies were not packed into the seat; the truck radio was not blaring some adolescent anthem from a best-forgotten decade; Budweiser was not being gulped from long neck bottles; and, most ominously, I was not being insulted or threatened.

Was I even on the right planet? Why had I even bothered lacing up my boots?

Oddly enough, the single man behind the wheel waived me over to his truck, "Hey buddy, wanna lift!"

When I reached the door the man even drew closer to the curb so that it would be easier for me to board. I took in the bed of the truck at a glance and saw that it was a working rig, with lots of loose bricks, some boards, a trowel, and a bucket. In less than a second I determined that this man was not a redneck runt stomper; but a working man.

The man was average height and extremely muscular; a definite mesomorphic body type, with square jaw. He looked a lot like the actor Robert Conrad. I guessed his age at about thirty. As I swung into the cab he extended his hand and said in a clear strong voice, "Hi, I'm Bruce. I'm a bricklayer, have been a heroin addict for eleven years, and am going to kill myself tonight."

I remember being able to feel the craggy splits in his dried out hands and trying to recall if my hands were currently cut from work as the heroin addict part of his introduction set in. As soon as I was seated he roared out into traffic, cutting off a car that had to swerve into the other lane. I nodded over my shoulder toward the swerving vehicle and his foot stomping the gas, "Bruce, a, you're not going to use the vehicle to kill yourself are you?"

He seemed offended, "Oh no man! I'm not like that. I'll get you wherever you're going safely. I just need to get some change so I can make a phone call."

As we rumbled down the street I handed over two quarters. He seemed happy, "Thanks man. Don't you wanna know who I'm calling?"

"It's none of my business. I'll give you some bills for gas when you drop me off."

He began to sound worried, "Aren't you going to try to talk me out of killing myself?"

"No."

"Why not?"

"You seem pretty serious."

"Well, that is what the change is for, so I can call my dad and have him unlock the door so I can get in and get my shotgun."

"Dude, don't do that!"

"So you don't want me to kill myself?"

"Look man, it's none of my business if you kill yourself. But you should use a thirty-eight or something."

"Really, I thought the shotgun would be more reliable."

"Look man, your dad is going to have to I.D. your body. You should at least leave the head on, alright."

"I hadn't thought about that. You know, that is real considerate."

I was looking around, noticing that we were headed farther downtown than I wanted to, "Hey man, I'm headed to Eastpoint..."

Over the centerline and up onto the concrete sidewalk we went, as Bruce did a hairpin u-turn onto Moravia. The truck was fishtailing as we headed east, but after he ground his wheel hub against the concrete median for a while he straightened out. Bruce was un-phased, "Hey man, there is a Dunkin' Doughnuts over there. Do you wanna get a doughnut?"

"Sure man."

The shotgun seemingly forgotten, we crossed Route 40 on the interstate ramp and were soon on North Point Blvd headed past Eastern Avenue. I observed, "Hey Bruce, that's it back there."

What was I thinking!

Bruce pulled a u-turn over the concrete median and was about to cut through the mall parking lot when he spotted a black chick in a nice new car waiting at the light; her peaceful commute home from work now a memory. He rumbled his truck right up besides her and screamed out the window, "Hey baby, you wanna date?"

She shook her head 'no' and said, "I have a boyfriend."

Bruce yelled, "So? Can I follow you home?"

I interjected, "Hey Bruce, her boyfriend probably looks like Bubba Smith, alright."

He regarded me with intense seriousness, "Really, you think so. She's kinna cute to have a big ugly boyfriend."

He then yelled down at her as she seemed to be considering running the red light, "Hey miss, my friend here says that your boyfriend probably looks like Bubba Smith. Is that so?"

She nodded 'yes' up at him with big frightened eyes, and Bruce looked over at me and grinned insanely, "Are you Jesus? You must be. You look like him and you know everything. I was thinking about going to church in the morning before killing myself—you wanna go to church with me?"

I sensed that it was time to take charge, "Doughnut; work; then, if you aren't dead yet, church in the morning."

Bruce seemed to experience an epiphany, "Why would I kill myself when I get to hang out with Jesus?"

"I guess that is the whole churchgoing point Bruce."

To recount the purchase of the doughnut, the theological debate that Bruce—now a devote Methodist I think—tried to start with the Pakistani doughnut clerk, and the scrawling of my work phone number on the greasy napkin with some woman's discarded lipstick, would, I think, take away from Bruce's moment of revelation.

Bruce never did call me at work the next morning so that I could announce my second coming to whichever lucky congregation he had planned on presenting me to. I would like to think though, that he ended up in church; in a suit that he put on himself.

The Streets Have Eyes #3: Claire, My Crack-head Cousin

© 2013 James LaFond

Claire

Claire is a former coworker of mine who I recently ran into at a bar—the bar I lived over top of 30 years ago when I moved to Baltimore. The place was owned by a pro football player back then. I remember that winter of 1981/82 being extremely cold, and with our utilities off—I think gas & electric payments were impinging on the beer fund—we were reduced to dragging railroad ties up out of the parking lot [where they were employed as car stops] and chopping them up on the living room floor to feed the fireplace, which did not have a functional flue; so if we stood up and breathed at the same time, we would die...

In any case, amid such stories of our youth, Claire related a recent harrowing one of her own that belongs in The Streets Have Eyes series. Before she gets on with her story, let me describe her as a short forty-something blonde who, decades ago, survived some brutal beatings at the hands and shoed feet of a man. She never let that slow her down and has done well in the workforce. A few years back we were working together after she had her knees replaced. Her job required her to walk up and down a long flight of stairs often. When her knees took a turn for the worse the employer added boxes of change [nickels, dimes, quarters, pennies] to her work load; I supposed to develop her hips as she gimped up the stairs.

Claire is one of those sensitive people who put up a tough front. She did not even let me know she was being 'sandbagged' with the coin-hauling chore so that the employer could get her off the payroll when she became totally disabled.

Overworking injured or sick employees is a venerable tradition in retail food, a practice I have fallen victim to also, when recovering from a spinal injury in my 30s.

Another coworker informed me of Claire's fate and I came up behind her on the stairs, "You should not be carrying that. You don't have any knees, its heavy, and this is an unsecured blind spot. No employee should haul money through here without an escort."

She chirped over her shoulder, "No sweat boss-man, nothing a little bone-on-bone can't take care of!" and continued up the stairs, waiving me off with a jerk of her little head as her joints creaked like loose floorboards.

So, when you read Claire's story, keep in mind that she's got the best tough act in town, and that fear doesn't control her like it does most people. She also makes a point of remembering hard times. She told me at the bar last Saturday that she had saved all of my disciplinary write-ups, as they had all made her cry, and was considering framing one. She did inform me as the interview kicked off that, as a boss, I had been "'a legendary hard-ass; Mister by the Book, jump through another hoop please!'"

"Now you're a writer, and you care!" [laughs]

My Crack-head Cousin

[A smart-phone picture of a short muscular, craggy-faced man of about 50, with a wide thick head, and a vacuous grin is presented as a narrative aid. The fellow looks like he could have been a pro boxer of the oft beaten but never stopped variety.]

"My crack-head cousin—he says he doesn't smoke anymore but he has COPD. He picks me up at ten in the morning for my Aunt Marge's funeral and as soon as I get in he cracks open a Budweiser longneck.

"I said, 'It's nice of you to pick me up' and he's just driving off drinking.

"So I'm like, 'I don't need this shit. Tell the truth, and choose your answer carefully. Are you picking me up because you want to, or because somebody told you to?'

"He's like, 'Well, um, I said I was goin' ta pick you up.'

"I said, 'Tell the truth.' And he said 'Well Aunt Pat asked me to.'

"We are headed through the tunnel and this state cop pulls up and he hides the beer. After we get through the tunnel he's chugging it and we get to the graveyard. We are at the graveyard and he's walking around stuffing this cake in his mouth that my Aunt Alice gave him, shoving it in his mouth with the palm of his hand—what a loser. I'm standing right on my grandfather's grave—may he rot in hell and burn for eternity! He molested me when I was a child. I should have spit on his grave.

"We get back into the car to cross back over from Glen Burnie and he is freaked about the tunnel and the cop, 'We aren't doin' the tunnel Claire. We're doin' the bridge.'

"So we are going around these back roads looking for the bridge. Of course he has his backup beer, the can of Bud Light that he pops open from out of the glove box. He tries to beat this one light and we almost get hit, and they're honking while we are in the intersection and I'm like, 'Oh my God! Is this how it's going to end?' Then he's got a lead foot and we are doing eighty on these side roads while he is drinking his beer.

"Besides, I knew he was on something. He says he doesn't do drugs anymore. But he watches our elderly aunt and uncle, and dispenses their medication—Oh he's getting his; eating perks and oxys out the ass probably.

"Now finally we are doing the bridge [The Key Bridge, which has a high apex and is shut down for wind speed occasionally.] and it is swaying—you can feel it move in the wind. And I hear this rattling.

Here he has the back door [passenger side] shut incompletely and it finally comes loose behind me and its banging on the guardrail—destroying this new car. Who the car belonged to I didn't even ask. I was yelling at him telling him to slow down and he is driving and drinking beer and reaching behind me to try and pull the door shut! Finally we make it over the bridge—whew!

"At least by this stage he is out of backup beer. We finally make it to the steak house and, guess what: the crack-head orders a beer. I thought I was never going to get home. But here I am, still kicking! There you go, a day with my family."

Joe-Damn!: A Harm City Snapshot

© 2013 James LaFond

Yesterday I interviewed a person I used to work with, who asked me about a mutual coworker. This brought back a flood of vivid images and words, as this man was a classic hoodlum-turned-curmudgeon.

His name was Joe, and he added the –Damn! whenever he wanted to make a manly point. Joe-Damn! had no fear, backed down from no one, not even 'bosses en big muvasuckas'. I met Joe-Damn! on the job when he was picking a fight with his supervisor, who towered over him menacingly. He had no racist sympathies and always stood up against what he thought was 'not right'. He changed employment often. Therefore our relationship was necessarily brief. The man did work. I can vouch for that.

What most endeared me to Joe-Damn! was the fact that he did not back down. He got into one scuffle with a racist white floor tech who was intentionally mopping over his new white shoes, and mumbling something about those shoes being too white for a black man to wear. When he dove for the redneck with the mop I grabbed the redneck and a black crew member grabbed Joe-Damn! who repeatedly exclaimed, "Damn! son let me at 'im so I can beat the race out a 'is ism!"

The redneck continued his insults until, after finding out that I—the only other white man there—was going to take sides with Joe-Damn! When this realization washed over his face he began to cry, out loud! I spent some time with my arm around him, letting him know that everything would be alright as soon as he got home to Redneck RFD, and was once again surrounded by racist bigots who would hate precisely as he did.

I returned to Joe-Damn! And inquired, "So are we cool know?"

He responded in his gravelly voice, "Damn! How can I even think about whoopin' a muvasucka who is cryin'? How'd you make his dumbass cry?"

"I don't hate black dudes. He can't deal with that—like a knife in his soul."

"Damn! you is a cruel muvasucka, turnin' on yo own like that! Sheeeit! Damn! Son! Fat liddle whiteboy all alone up in hea—knows it now—ole-no-hatin' Jimmy throwin' his pasty ass to the bruthas!"

After that, Joe-Damn! and I were fast friends. He had a liking for the ladies, but lacked the sophistication necessary for courtship. Once, when we were punching in, we walked past Ebony, a willowy dark-skinned babe with short greased-down hair, in heels and tight jeans, who weighed perhaps 90 pounds. Joe-Damn! stopped, looked her up and down and around, spun on his heel, looked at her tight jeans again, looked at me, looked at her petite breasts, looked away, and then finally looked at her face, and said, "Damn!"

Ebony then looked at me as I 'nodded' hello to her and asked, "What the hell is his problem?"

Joe-Damn! then spread his arms, expanded his chest, took to one knee with backswept hands as if ready to serenade a princess up in a chastity tower, and said, "Damn! Don' you know that I love your fine ass, you beautiful bald black bitch!"

Ebony just looked at him with disgust, looked at me with amazement, and said in a huff as she walked by me, "You can jus' take his ghetto ass back where you found it!"

Now, what did Joe say to that?

He stood up, shook his head, and said, "Damn! son, that shit was cold—been workin' on the delivery all week!"

Off we went to work.

Considering Joe-Damn's lack of polish it came as no surprise that he did not get along well with the big bull dyke that worked in seafood, who claimed Ebony as part of her 'babe stable'. I forget the lesbian lady's name, but Joe-Damn! had his own name for her, 'Silvaback.'

One evening I came to work and was informed that 'Silvaback' had been fired for cussing out a customer. An hour or so later Joe-Damn! and I were in the back aisle breaking down freight. We had had no discussion as to the fate of his rival for Ebony's affection. To illustrate how Joe-Damn! communicated in a bard-like way, rather than as a manner of discourse, I leave you with the last words I heard from him, just days before he was fired for fighting a coworker in front of the off duty cop that stood guard while the manager closed down the ghetto grocery store.

Thus Spake Joe-Damn! Upon the Virtues of Womanhood

Each line in the following passage was preceded by a long look at the seafood case, and a harsh snort or a damn! as the bard lifted cases of detergent onto a six-wheeled U-boat.

"Invincible dyke bitch?"

"Hah!"

"Invincible pussy-eatin' dyke bitch?"

"Hah!"

"Invincible ugly pussy-eatin' dyke bitch?"

"Hah!"

"Invincible fat uglay pussy-eatin' dyke bitch?"

"Hah!"

"Invincible silva-backed fat uglaay pussy-eatin' dyke bitch?"

"Invincible shit! Hah!!"

"Yeah Silvaback, how much pussy you eatin' now with nary a paycheck?"

"Not a patch! Hah!!"

If someone knows where Joe-Damn! is could we please get him lined up for an appearance on reality TV?

The Streets Have Eyes #4: "Ad Da Speed A Fright!"

© 2013 James LaFond

When one resides, as I do, in the armpit of the Eastern United States in the societal secretion gland of Baltimore, there is never-the-less, occasional cause to celebrate the beautiful night with a stroll down quiet county lanes. I prefer lanes with sidewalks and without Dodge Ram-mounted rednecks. Last night I split the difference and went into the night under a starry blue sky out in Redneckville to enjoy the cool aftermath of a day of downpours.

This was a calculated act of selfishness, and I had no plans on gathering Harm City lore for this lurid page. However, as oft-stated in this not-so-hallowed space, I am a man of science; a professional writer never without a pen or two on my person. I had forgotten my notebook—any book will do really— and dragooned my left forearm into service as a most uncooperative piece of parchment.

I was strolling down the right side of a westbound road. This road had modest frame houses on the left, and an overgrown tangle of twenty year old woods along the uninhabited right side, which was once home to a housing project that looked like a 1950s motel. That eyesore is thankfully providing root footage for the plants that are reclaiming this defiled land where I once saw a man being batted into traction by three baseball bat wielding debt collectors. Things thankfully have changed for the better at that particular Harm City coordinate. But lo and behold, up the street a ways, heading my way on the uninhabited side was one—no two—figures.

I casually observed the oncoming duo as they were men, and men on foot always bear watching. Just ask the Baltimore City cop that was shadowing me this morning as I strolled along reading in the ghetto. About a hundred yards out I could see clearly each figure. I was unable to determine if they were together or even communicating. They were both speaking.

The man in the front eyed me boldly as he bounced along like a Chicom infantryman from 1951 dogging a column of Marines. He was just under six feet and just over 200 pounds. He wore camo cargo shorts and a camo wife beater, hauled a new backpack, and bounced along on new athletic shoes. His ball cap was also of Blackwater approved urban camo and covered a cleanly shaved head. There were three curious things about him: he made hard eye-contact with me from a Terry Bradshaw pass away; carried a cloth-covered bundle over his shoulder that was ten feet long and seemed to conceal either PVC tubing, long closet dowel rods, or Achilles' two favorite battle spears; and he chanted something of a marching tune. If Donald Trump decided to go on safari in America's largest trailer park, this guy would be his luggage porter...and I suppose that I would be his translator.

I shall now type the marching verse I copied onto my arm in blue ink so I can take a shower. Before considering this masterful performance, keep in mind that he chanted loudly and to no one, and in no direction, in particular. Whether he was chanting to me; the stumblebum behind him; or to the hood-rat ghosts he clearly saw peopling the sidewalk in front of their former domiciles, must be left to your imagination. The one man marching band boomed a line with every second step.

"Loog oud Holmes!

"A regonin' iz commin'!

"Ad da speed a fright man!

"Ninedy miles an hour;

"Rogedin' [rocketing] block—a concrete storm!

Walg on behine dis shid..."

By that point he was out of clear hearing and continuing briskly on his way.

Next up was the stumblebum; a towering thin man with wide boney shoulders and a square head covered with shaggy black hair, dressed in jeans and flannel. This fellow was having better luck with side-to-side locomotion than forward. As I came abreast of him he hugged a telephone pole like a drowning man, looked across the street at me, and did what else, but panhandle! Regular readers are well acquainted with my dislike of panhandlers. However, I was moved by this man briefly as he hugged his savior pole and looked covetously at me—despite my ten year old clothes—seemingly a 'pillar' of his community.

The tall leaning drunk nodded before beginning his delivery:

"Eggshuze me sirrr.

"Hey pal?

"Sirrr, do you thig you coul' spare twelve cent?"

I responded, "Nah man, I'm broke."

He waived and mumbled, "Ogay man, dage 'are..."

He continued to mumble as he staggered on.

In case I thought my weird walk was over I soon came upon a young hip hopster in the right lane of this suburban road; shirtless, pants around his knees to expose his gray briefs, hat cocked to the side. This reminder of the artist formerly known as Fifty Cent was washing his car at night. As he polished his rear fender he looked up at me, put his cigarette to his lips, and took a long thoughtful drag. He then blew a smoke kiss at me with a dark narrow look.

I just nodded courteously and headed for the nearest open business. What else was there to do but get off of that road? Besides, my parchment was all filled in.

If you Harm City readers have any theories as to the bundle hauled by the nocturnal road poet, just sign in below and have at it.

James 6/14/13

The Streets Have Eyes #5: Nasty Norman & the Carryout Girl

© 2013 James LaFond

Two weeks ago I was having breakfast with a college student who is working as a manager trainee at a pizza carryout. He tells it better than I could.

"About six o'clock Thursday this crippled fat person pulled up [in an old dark SUV.] He was a nasty fat white person, probably lives in a trailer with some kind of nasty dog—probably folds up the whole pizza and eats it like a hot pocket."

Author: "Okay, so this dude is so nasty that his hypothetical domestic canine is guilty by association; by definition 'nasty' in an irredeemable 'Hills Have Eyes' kind of way?"

[Laughter]

"Yes. But there is no way that this guy's nasty dog is as cool as the dog in the movie. This would be a homeless red-neck mutant dog."

Author: "Do you realize that this is the single most damning personal judgment I have recorded in over a decade?"

"This guy was old—not as old as you, but looked a lot older—and fat, and had no shirt on, and had three breasts. I don't know what the boob in the middle was, but it was nasty and jiggled like the rest. A third man-boob, how much more nasty can you get? His hair was greasy and he was scruffy."

"He hobbled out of his nasty SUV—which was not nasty per say, just worn-out and overworked, especially on the driver's side. He had to run four-hundred to four-fifty—a definite chair-melter. He had this fast food cup with tea in it—no ice. As he was limping to the door the girl that was manning the counter fled into the bathroom."

"The other girl stepped up to the counter to help him and he asks for ice. He does not want to buy anything, just wants free ice for his warm tea. We don't sell fountain sodas and have no ice maker. It is a hundred degrees in there. We sell bottled sodas out of coolers. If we had ice we would have given him some just to get rid of him. He asks three times and still does not take 'no' for an answer. I stepped away to check on something and when I turned around he was gone but had spilled his tea all over the counter. Apparently his tea had no value without a free supply of ice."

"He then sat in his SUV for fifteen minutes, blocking the delivery men from coming and going. We were about to call the police when he pulled off. When he left the girl came out of the bathroom. When I asked her what that was about she told me that he had come in before and offered her money to dance for him, to dance with his peg-leg as a pole! She was scared to death of this guy. He is a peg-legged pervert!"

The Streets Have Eyes #6: The Tao of Captain Backwash

© 2013 James LaFond

Two weeks ago I was in a mixed-race bar seated between the blacks and the whites—the United Nations representative in that inebriated little world. To my right sat the middle-aged Michael Jordan look-alike who was working his way into the fat girl across the bar one shot of tequila at a time. To my left was 'Get a Room', the forty-something drunk stoner couple who shoot dope in the alley, step into the bar to chug beer by the bucket, and then neck and dry-hump in the walkway, doing their best to give monogamy a bad name. The aging ho with the high-heel earrings is not on station so it has not become a sleaze-fest yet.

The drive up muggings have apparently abated in this area, as I'm not getting any interview leads, so I'm about ready to pack it in. Then a tall long-haired brunette of a girly man with a long aquiline nose and the scruffiest beard a testosterone deficient post-apocalyptic hippie can manage, walks in—

dressed like Captain Morgan! The Captain has it all: knee high boots, broad belt, hat, open long-tailed jacket—and a sword.

The Captain, at six-four and a buck-sixty, stands imperiously behind Get a Room. The dyke barmaid asks if he needs anything and he gives her a raised eye-brow and finger, that I think meant, 'Hold your fire until we are astern boys'. She returns to chilling glasses. Get a Room take a break from their unsuccessful procreation efforts and beginning heckling The Captain, "Ahoy matey', 'Arrgh, rum' and then perform a duet rendition of a song with a chorus about men sitting on a dead man's chest.

The Captain remained aloof and silent, so the female component of Get a Room said, "Hey we're talking pirate to you."

The Captain stepped behind me and sneered, "No self-respecting pirate would use such low order speech. We are the nobility of the Seven Seas."

The pirate song resumes from Get a Room to my left as they are joined by an annihilated redneck up front, who reminds them that it was bottles that were on the dead man's chest.

Michael to my right takes his focus off the overstuffed white spandex across the bar long enough to whisper to me, "Dude has a sword!"

The Captain than waives over the barmaid.

She asks, "What 'ill it be hon?"

"A shot."

"A shot of what?"

He turns his head in a measured way, as if he is used to being disappointed by his wait staff, and sneers, "Rum."

"What kind of rum?"

He disdains to answer and Get a Room comes to the rescue, chiming in with both sets of pipes at the same time, "Captain Morgan!"

The Captain nods his ascent as he hooks his thumbs into his broad belt. When the shot comes he counts out coin, including pennies, to pay for it. He then takes the shot against the rail behind Michael and begins to sip menacingly with one boot back against the wall. Michael looks at me with his shoulders hunched forward and head ducked, as if he is expecting to be stabbed in the back, "What the fuck!?!"

I just nodded at The Captain, and Michael, getting my meaning, turns, "Hey Captain is that a real sword?"

The Captain then draws what seems to me to be some kind of straight single-edged boarding sword, with a cup hilt, about 20 inches long. Michael whispers, "Jesus, time for me to expedite matters."

Michael moves to the other side of the bar and buys more top shelf tequila for the fat girl and begins whispering in her ear. I am left with The Captain, who finishes his rum at a measured pace and then strolls out to a cheer of "Arrgh matey" from Get a Room and their white trash cohorts.

I was left wondering about the eccentric Captain for nearly a week, until I was taking an early morning walk through the alleys and back streets near the bar and noticed him in standard hippie regalia, his long hair in a peace-and-love ponytail, and a guitar in his hand. He was headed to the main corner to set up and play for change.

The Streets Have Eyes

When I passed him again a few moments later he was going through the high-volume trash bin on the corner where he would play, retrieving discarded bottles of soda, water, and tea, and drinking what was left—after, of course, he checked for any floating cigarette butts.

A man must have his standards after all.

James, 9/5/13

The Streets Have Eyes #7: NEBO Nose

© 2013 James LaFond

It was about this time of year, some 18 years past. I had worked the overnight job and the morning job out in Eastern Baltimore County, had journeyed down into Dundalk to work the afternoon job, and was heading home through Highland on the #23. I changed busses at the Highland Café—which was anything but a café—and boarded the #22 for the ascent to Northeast Baltimore. It was a cold windy day, which always kicked up paper trash and swirled it around.

I took one of the last remaining seats toward the front, as the back was packed with hood-rats. People were already standing in the aisle. There was a reason why this seat had been left open. The first thing you do is touch the seat and make sure it has not been pissed on. The seat was dry. The reason for it being unoccupied was seated by the window next to it.

I never knew his name. The kids called him Nose. He wore torn hospital scrubs and tattered slippers underneath of a large oversized nylon coat which he had stuffed with newspapers. He smelled, but it was 30 degrees out. He wasn't ripe in that oily homeless fashion that famously knocks people off of park benches from ten yards up wind on hot summer days. He was a white man of about fifty with a bald pate that gave way to stringy once-brown hair impregnated with filth and grease a few seasons old. This mass of hair lay rigidly like plastic flowers on the grease-darkened collar of his dumpster coat. Where a beard should have been were healed sores, with scabs lingering on the downy remnants of a once manly beard, now reduced to a feathery mange-like consistency.

I nodded off on the over-warm bus. Baltimore bus drivers are famous for cranking the heat on a bus up high enough to keep them warm in their 'weather seat' upfront. This roasts the rest of the people out. And, if you have been punched in the nose thousands of times, your nose will then begin to run in the unnatural heat, necessitating the need for a tissue in your pocket to dab the beaten down nostril in question.

Just before we hit Route Forty a dozen more students got on. This was a fully packed 'school bus', with sixty-five to seventy bodies on a tube provided with 45 seats. Two pretty little girls got on the bus. I stood so that one could have a seat. As I began to move to the back, Nose seemed to have also been of a chivalrous frame of mind, as he too rose and gave up his seat. The two girls squeaked their thanks and took their prissy little seats, chattering away about their day. Nose nodded wearily to me, seeming to feel good that we two loan white men had shown these thirty black boys how to behave.

Nose, was not however, up to shouldering his way through the tightly packed hood-rats as I did, racking faces with the shoulder flap of my duster, and stepping on little sneakered feet with my work boots. I got to the pole at the back door as the bus pulled off and headed up Edison Highway. [Read Rat Ratification, about 100 articles down on this page, for a description of the rat-infested field spanned by the Edison Highway Bridge, where the famous battle was fought by the train tracks.]

More students got on. Nose was hemmed in between a mass of standing teens, holding on to the overhead bar, and kind of gently rocking and swaying with the motion of the bus. Nose was having a hard time staying awake in the heat of the bus. He also had another problem. He sneezed from his swaying stupor, spraying the dainty damsels—coifed in yellow, white and pink—with the effluvia born of weeks sleeping on the cold streets of Harm City.

The girls screeched and made 'oo' sounds, and wiped each other off with the fuzzy cuffs of their jacket sleeves. Nose nodded back off, lolling like a baby being rocked in its carriage as the overloaded bus rocked over the bridge. Then a young hood-rat next to me pointed with his chin and said to his friend, "Yo, check out Nose—shit be nasty up in hea!"

I looked to see a good double strand of greenish biomass stretching from the nostrils of Nose, for a length, of, let's say: two inches. Some girl behind the two dainties tapped the near one on the shoulder and pointed up at the alien life from descending from the street-weary naval cavities, a mere foot above her $200 hair weave! The girl looked up and squeaked, cringing over against her friend, with no room to squeeze out of the seat.

The two hood-rats next to me, obviously not favored suitors of these two young ladies, enjoyed the show with snickering smirks.

Then Nose sneezed again and the strands of goo actually held. As the girls squealed and hugged each other like teenage horror movie victims, the tenacious green slime strands lengthened to a hand span and intertwined into one yo-yoing biomass. Those standing around Nose attempted to squeeze away, forcing him forward. He was somehow holding on with his hands half asleep, as he swayed over the girls, who hugged and screeched in horror as the oozing snake of green slime wiggled, swung, lengthened, and contracted, according to the movement of the bus and the labored breathing of Nose.

The near girl had her head jammed under the other girl's protective arm, while the girl in the window seat looked up in horror at the swinging mess and began to panic, "Oh ma Gawd yo. We needs a Kleenex up in hea."

The bus hit a bump and Nose lurched forward as we began heading down into the Belair Edison Neighborhood. The hands of Nose miraculously held onto the overhead bar, the nasal discharge now lengthened ridiculously as both girls broke into screams. The bus then banked onto Erdman Avenue causing Nose and some of those around him to lean-fall into the passengers beneath him.

The hood-rats besides me were saying, "Yo dis shit be hilarious!"

Plaintive cries for a "Kleenex, napkin, paper—or sumptin'!" could be heard from the front of the bus. I had lost sight of the comedy as I offloaded at my stop and laughed out loud, the best laugh I can ever remember having.

I saw Nose a week or so later on the #15, huddled up front in a bomber jacket sneezing and drooling among the old ladies returning from their shopping trips. I have not seen him since.

The Streets Have Eyes #8: Denizen Cane on The Bus of Heaven

© 2013 James LaFond

12/18-19/2013, 11:00 p.m. to 12:10 a.m.

I bussed it into the ghetto on the way to work last night to check on the homeless—as I am so concerned about their accommodations. One dude was sleeping in the gutter in the mouth of a steaming sewer. Another dude was curled up in a ball against a brick wall under the awning of a pawn shop. There were some drunks walking around. I got my connect—no problem.

12:10

When I stepped on the bus there was an open seat if only this one fetal drunk in overalls would sit up. Somehow, as I made him move and he mumbled, he managed to remain prone on the one seat.

There was one dude up front chatting up the bus driver, and leaning against the dash, in violation of the federal ordinance posted above their heads. Everything was normal.

Then, at Kane and Eastern, Smokey, a small middle-aged man in a bomber jacket and ski cap, stepped up with his cane in one hand, and his bedding in the other [a plastic bag full of circulars and newspapers that he covers up with]. Smokey has a dark patina rather than a complexion, from those years of unbathed nights warming his hands over a trash bin fire. Smokey was also smoking a long brown, and much sucked on, cigarette.

12:22

I was thinking, 'Here I go again. Three white dudes on the bus: me, a drunk, and a homeless guy.'

The bus driver said, "Put that cigarette out. You ain't stinkin' my bus up."

Smokey stops a little as if his back is stiff, and kind of grimaces, almost biting the cigarette in half. He did not, however, stop smoking.

The bus driver said, "Put that cigarette out befo' you stink my bus up!"

Smokey puts the cigarette out on the collar of his jacket and said, proudly, as if addressing us all, "That's alright I just shit myself!"

He stepped back toward us—not having paid—and the driver said, "Oh, no he didn't!"

A big lady sitting to his left and my right covered her face with her scarf and said, "Oh yes he did!"

The driver pulled off, as if speed would save her nose. I was now digging frantically for pen and note pad.

Smokey then smiled at the ceiling and stepped over to sit down across from the scarf-veiled lady, between two young people—who bolted for the back of the bus. As he turned to face the lady across from whom he was about to sit, he smiled at her. "This bus is heaven to me. I love this bus. God bless you people—smell the love!"

The scarf-veiled lady said, "You are nastay. You should get off this bus."

Smokey plopped down on his seat with a smile. "This is some nasty shit ain't it. You want a smell? You want to wipe my ass?"

The lady then crossed her arms in front of her face and peered at him in disgust as I broke into laughter and had a hard time keeping pen to paper.

Smokey continued to speak loudly, firm, and clear, with nearly perfect courtroom diction, "This bus is so warm, like heaven. I got kicked out of the bar earlier for pissing myself. I've been so cold. You people don't realize how painful it is to shit out in this freezing cold. Would you let me shit in your house Miss?"

The lady cringed behind her scarf as my eyes ran with tears laughing at the insanity. The lady fired back from behind her scarf, "You stink, get your smelly self off the bus so people can breathe."

Smokey laid back and grinned with his brown teeth. "Oh, I can breathe just fine! I'll see you in church!"

The bus driver stopped the bus where Northpoint Blvd loops around Eastern in a cloverleaf, and demanded he get off the bus.

Smokey [knowing that odor is not an off-putting cause] inquired, "For what reason?"

"For being disrespectful!"

"I'm staying on this nice warm bus—smell the love people!"

"I'll call the cops!"

"Good, they will take me to another warm place."

I was still laughing. But the rest of the people began to complain about getting home late. The dude that had been chatting the driver up reminded her that Smokey had not paid, so she demanded he come up and show his ticket.

Smokey stood, shook his hips a little, and waddled toward the front, the veiled lady pinching her nose and pointing with squeals of disgust at a large lump above the back of his knee.

12:30

As Smokey was going through all of the trash in his wallet the man stepped down the stairs, and off the bus. Smokey continued to fuss for a pass that was not apparently there. As the driver began to question him with her nose in the sleeve of her sweater, two big brown hands reached up and grabbed Smokey's jacket and hurled him out onto the grassy median of the cloverleaf.

The big man bounded onto the bus to a round of applause. The driver was stunned. "What did you do?"

He said, "Baby, drive, I don't work fo' no MTA. I wanna ged home. En Lord knows what be crawlin' up out a him next—roll!"

She rolled as directed.

For the next ten minutes I watched Smokey's lonely cane rattle where it was propped up against the befouled seat of its onetime master, not a pace from my seat, next to the drunk who slept through the entire thing.

The Streets Have Eyes #9: The Fate of Denizen Cane

© 2013 James LaFond

My man Smokey showed up where I worked five hours after he was thrown from the Bus of Heaven by the Standee Line Dude. He was staring in the window at Bubba, our giant cashier, who became fearful and summoned management, who made him leave with much finger-pointing ado.

This morning, Saturday, December 21, 2013, at 3:40 a.m., I was breaking down my frozen food order when I saw Smokey standing in front of the deli counter waiving a canister of whipped-topping at the ladies behind the counter and making rank propositions concerning the nozzle and the contents.

When I pointed out to the crew that this little man was the famous bus defecator and homeless prophet from Kane Street, they kept their distance in case he was primed for another scent-worthy sermon. [You know Diogenes the Cynic [meaning

74

'dog'] was an ancient Greek philosopher who famously squatted and did his business at the end of a speech at the Isthmian Games at Corinth.]

Then, as Nokia was trying to count his teeth from the other side of the counter, a Baltimore Country cop happened by the deli for his lunch. He promptly wrinkled up his nose, went to the night captain, and asked if he wanted Smokey gone. The last I saw of Smokey was him backing up out the front door, arguing with the very tall cop who followed him, and craning his neck backward uncomfortably, even leveling a gnarly finger at the Pontius Pilate in blue who had interrupted his whipped-topping miracle.

The Streets Have Eyes #10: Coversatin' With Car

© 2014 James LaFond

Yesterday I spoke to a college student who spent all day Sunday in Washington D.C. attending museums by day and watching the Washington Wizards get slaughtered by the Golden State Warriors at the Verizon Center into the evening. He was very much impressed with how different D.C. was from Baltimore. But some things never change in America's urban landscape. This is what he had to say:

"It was nice and clean, but there were a huge number of homeless guys, sleeping all over the place. The police did not hassle them at all. [Sounds like Homeless Eden.] Mack and Villie and I were walking buy this one little guy on the sidewalk outside of the Verizon Center. The man was in his mid-fifties with a white beard. He was small and thin. Mack is six-seven. This guy looks at Mack and says, "Hey White Dick, I'm a badass nigga taday!"

"It was so uncalled for, and so funny. The guy just kept walking. We were calling Mack, 'White Dick' all night long. Not only were there no bums getting hassled by cops, but the bums did not beg—not one request for change. They just slept.

"The most astonishing thing I think I ever saw was this one guy on a side street just screaming at this car, having a full on conversation with it. We really didn't want to get close enough to hear exactly what he was saying. But he seemed to believe that the car was talking back to him."

There you have a suburban Marylander's view of D.C. If I were mayor of Baltimore I'd let our bums know how sweet it is down the road—even circulate a brochure—and start launching greyhound bus loads of Harm City panhandlers at the Capital of the World.

'You People': A Moronic Taste of Harm City

© 2014 James LaFond

This is just one afternoon as a writer among the illiterate; a two hour slice of my writing life. Erique has postulated that I have an 'inappropriate aura' that I 'bring out the weirdness in people'. After yesterday I am inclined to at least consider his suggestion. But then again, maybe it is Baltimore. It seems when NFL players move to Baltimore they begin getting in trouble with the law, especially when they vacation out of town, as if that Harm City mojo clings to them like avarice to politicians.

Ray Rice, uber-geeky-good-guy in glasses with an 'I love Mom' smile, is a standout Public Relations man for the NFL, devoting much energy to an anti-bullying campaign. Yesterday, just before heading out for this little pre-training excursion, I viewed a video of Ray dragging the body of his unconscious wife-to-be—who he had just knocked out in the elevator—into a hallway and dropping her on her face! Since Ray is my mother's favorite football player I will come to his defense on reflex and postulate that perhaps he was just applying an anti-bullying technique. You know that black women do initiate more violence in Baltimore than men. Perhaps he was just defending himself against those lethal designer fingernails he paid $500 to have installed on his personal nagging and bitching machine?

I don't know if it will fly Mom, but I tried for your boy RayRay, here.

3:45, Harford Road & Northern Parkway

I am sitting in the back corner of a transit bus loaded with 40 or so junior high school and high school kids. I try to field a phone call but could not hear the caller. Fully half of the vocabulary in use begins with the letters n, f, b and y. Spitting on the bus is rampant. One nerd is caught in an alpha male's seat and is made to sit next to the creepy old white guy in the trench coat. When my stop comes up on Loch Raven and Taylor I accidentally elbow a beta male in the head and step on the alpha's foot, squeeze past a fat girl and a skinny kid, and manage to get off in time to sprint and catch the #3 bus going out to Cromwell Bridge Road.

Having survived that heart attack scare I board the #3 and offload at the Whiz Carwash and walk up to the karate school where I coach this doll of a Russian chick on how to slash and stab men. If Putin met her he'd fire some American news anchor and get her a spot on RT.com, broadcasting online to frustrated Libertarian news junkies...

4:45, Loch Raven Boulevard & Joppa Road

Anna and I are waiting to cross Joppa to the diner to discuss a writing project. Behind us a tall boy in his late teens is listening to our conversation. He chimes in, "Excuse me Miss are you foreign? I heard your accent. You sound foreign!"

Anna smiles somewhat uncomfortably as we begin to cross.

"Excuse me, Ma'am, are you foreign?"

"Yes, I am. Aren't we all, in a way?"

"Yeah, well, I just heard an accent. Where are you from?"

"Take a guess!"

"Oh I'm terrible at guessing... um. Norway?"

"(impressed) Pretty close, actually!"

"Really? Is it Scandinavian? Finland?"

"A little further to the east."

"Sweden? No? I give up, I don't know."

"Russian."

"Oh Russian! It' a cool accent. You're my first foreigner. There's mostly white guys around."

"Really? Foreigners are all over the place."

"I met an Iranian but didn't talk to him."

The boy now passes us and is walking backwards with his hands in his pockets talking, a childish light in his eyes. "I met an Iranian—they're all over the place! But I did not talk to him. I talked to you. I want to meet new foreigners and talk to them. Thank you Miss."

By now Anna was genuinely smiling as we walked up to an unpromising Bel Loc Diner, made famous in a Berry Levinson movie titled Diner. The Bel Loc was once opened 24 hours. A few years back it was opened until 11:00 pm. Now, the sign says, it closes at 3 pm.

5:00 pm, Subway Sandwiches, Joppa Road

We have jaywalked, slush-slogged and ice-walked to this sandwich shop where only two other patrons are seated eating. Just as the two small polite people behind the counter hand us our cups and food and we begin to step away, one of the patrons, a towering black man in his twenties, rises and pats his belly. As we step away he seems to have an epiphany and blurts to the 4' 10" brunette behind the counter, "Now I know why you people are so tiny! You don't stuff yourselves and over fill your belly's like we do."

Anna gave me this 'Oh My God' look and the guy behind the counter shakes his head in apparent embarrassment. The little lady behind the counter is not put off though. She says, "Yes, you people are big! Very big, much eating!"

The man, seemingly justified in his theory says, "We're big because we overfill ourselves. We should eat sensibly like you little Asians."

The little brunette then grins and points to her head, "Yes, but we have big mind!"

By now we are at the table and Anna is saying, "Oh My. I have learned more about Baltimore today than I have in the past decade."

I reminded her that such were the benefits of slumming in my company.

The Streets Have Eyes #11: Tiny Dancer

© 2014 James LaFond

I remember her as a 45 pound child, just 4 years ago. Since 2010 I have caught the bus at 10:30 pm on this busy Baltimore City primary street in front of her mother's house.

I see her mother come and go in her mini-van.

I see her mother's man come home from work in his utility van.

I saw her older sister get dropped off in a fancy dress by a man that appeared to be her grandfather.

Her middle brother often plays with their family dog in the back yard and dutifully sets out the trash.

Her older brother walks past me with his friends and nods good evening, a quiet mild-mannered teenager, not some trifling fool.

Just like the rest of her family, 'Tiny' has responsibilities. She walks her older sister's baby in the carriage. A young woman, who might be an aunt or a cousin, visits on occasion. When it is time for her to go, 'Tiny' waits for the bus with her, loads the young lady's luggage on the bus, and then runs across the street to the family home.

So, what is troubling me?

I believe she is between 14 and 16. She is four feet ten inches tall and perhaps 85 pounds, with an extremely athletic build. She seems to have what my grandmother called 'that jumping bean energy' that some high metabolism people are blessed with.

What troubles me about 'Tiny' is that she dances in the street. She gets out there about two feet off the curb and dances in the headlights like a junior high school hip hop honey. This past Tuesday night, for ten full minutes, she put on a show for the oncoming motorists, some of whom honked their horns appreciatively. This happens 50 yards from a house full of her family members who seem to be living a nice lower middle-class life on the Harm City line. I suppose they are inside hypnotized by their various electronic devices while she goes about her more primitive life out of doors.

I averted my eyes during most of the performance, her obviously being a child. She seemed to be working very hard to correctly execute various maneuvers. There was nothing slutty about it really—but rather weirdly athletic. In some other context perhaps it would be an appropriate art form. I really do not know what to think, not having crucial information such as whether or not her mother knows what she is doing out there in the gutter at 10:30 pm on a school night. Whenever I see her do this I kind of grin inside at her outgoing nature, even as the context of her anonymous American Idol street audition saddens me.

The Streets Have Eyes #12: Do the Bright Thing, Not the Right Thing

© 2014 James LaFond

My street has a halfway house for drug addicts every 10 doors. These houses are occupied by 5 to 15 stoners, many put into these dwellings by court order. I know one delightful young lady who operates such a house the next street over.

"When I took over they had just fumigated for bed bugs and had moved in all new mattresses with plastic covers. But those things burrow into wood and the floor boards had an inch of filth all the way around. I don't mind cleaning, but how do you do heavy cleaning with that much traffic. We have two attractive girls and nine guys. They have dated them all.

"So, my second day in I piss test them all, and they all fail—every one of them. Out they go. I had the entire week to clean that place, and I needed it. I got all the crude and gunk cleaned up. Typically I'm putting one out a week."

With some background behind us, let us look over the gables of my plantation five doors down to the left, to that recovery house, not the one three doors up to my right. This house is occupied by 1 young lady and almost 10 men, mostly in their 20s. One of them failed his piss test, and was put out yesterday at 4:30 p.m. with his three plastic shopping bags worth of possessions.

My cutest roommate, who I shall refer to as Mary Poppins, knocked on my door and informed me that, since she was leery of having this dude nodding out on the curb and getting splattered [wishful thinking that was on my part] by a speeding SUV thumbing along under rap-power, she had asked him to sit in the driveway of the vacant next door. She just wanted me to have my Neanderthal radar out incase Harm City punished her for doing a good deed.

I looked out the window and saw this tall able-bodied youth sullenly sitting against the side of the vacant behind some cast off ghetto furniture with ashtray upholstery, as if some Godforsaken nation had failed to motivate him and that terminal ennui had set in; as if, well, as if he were stuck in postmodern America.

Mary Poppins went outside and gave him a cup of water as he seemed hot and thirsty. The manchild did have the dignity not to beg, and assured her that his mother was on his way up from the Washington D.C. vicinity to rescue him.

Twenty minutes later Marry Poppins looked outside and saw, to her horror, that he was passed out on the asphalt and something wet was staining the surface next to him. She was afraid that maybe he had cut himself. She went outside and saw that he had used the water she had provided him to cook up some heroin and shoot up!

The needle was still in his arm when he hit the pavement and fell out beside him.

My man!

Make room, brother, make room!

Despite my notable lack of empathy, Mary did her civic duty and called 911 for an ambulance. The ambulance was in no hurry and the 911 operator was interrogating Mary as if she had something to do with the overdose. The operator demanded that she stay on the phone, communicate with the 'victim' and be on hand to administer aid and file a police report. This made Mary feel very uncomfortable. So she 'removed herself from the situation' despite her 'nagging guilt for having supplied the water' and retreated into our house. There she consulted with the first guest to arrive for the evening, the lawyer who verifies the immigration paperwork for my visiting female groupies from Bangkok, Ulan Bator, and Barcelona.

He advised her to 'stay inside, to 'not get involved', to 'not have any more communication with the 911 operator', and to 'absolutely not permit her personal information to appear on the police report'.

The paramedics did arrive in time to revive the 'victim'. His mother was not far behind. I suppose she'll find him in her basement one day, with a needle hanging out of his arm like Mary Poppins did yesterday.

In the Narcostate—particularly in its Number one heroin user zone—doing the right thing is very often not the bright thing. Drug addicts and urban people in particular, are generally looking for a free score and are constantly bombarded with advertisements for ambulance chasing lawyers. There are two different versions of the proverbial 'pot of gold' at the end of the Narcostate rainbow: the lottery, and the lawsuit.

Be careful out there.

The Streets Have Eyes #13: The Vengeance of Denizen Kane

Warning: Do not read this before or during your meal.

© 2014 James LaFond

I believe Denizen Kane was once a lawyer, before he went completely insane. He does speak with the diction of a man who has spent decades as an inmate of higher learning institutions. He stands a meager five feet and two inches, weighs about 120 pounds, has keen beady eyes, a sharp nose, and tends to wear a wicked grin on his pointed chin. His hair is graying and neatly cropped. He dresses well and lightly for a homeless guy.

Denizen Kane can be found lurking along Eastern Avenue from East Baltimore around Highlandtown, all the way out to Chase, where the area's only functioning drive-in movie graces the waterfront. I can well imagine Denizen Kane has carved out a roost for his funky self somewhere in the weed's around Bengie's drive-in, viewing free films and committing the odd olfactory atrocity.

The last time we saw Denizen Kane at work was in the wee hours of a winter morning, a mere week or so after 'spreading the love' on the Bus of Heaven. On that morning he was ejected from the store by a cop who just happened in to buy his lunch at the deli, and ran into Denizen Kane waxing obscene.

He's back!

John had just gotten back from vacation yesterday. As much as he hates using the men's room, as it is routinely befouled by the indigent homeless debri that resides in that node of the Armpit of the East Coast, he had to go. So in he went. It did not reek too badly yet. Our Brazilian floor tech had just hosed it down and scrubbed it.

John does not know Denizen Kane, but taking into account John's recollection of the mysterious bathroom intruder's oratory skills and his appearance as glimpsed through the crack in the single stall, I have determined that he was victimized by our diabolical homeless superhero.

Let's have it from John in his own words:

"You know, sometimes you have to go. No sooner do I sit down than this little old dirtball guy comes in and says, 'Hey man, I need to get in there—I have to go!'

"I say, 'Look Pal, I just sat down. If it's that bad go knock on the women's room door and use one of their stalls. They have two.'

"By this time he's already grunting, 'Sorry sir, it's too late!'

"Then I see the shit start hitting the floor as he's cheering himself on, and trying to get his short ass over the trash can [which is three feet high] with his pants down around his ankles. Shit's hitting the floor, getting caught up in his pants, getting flung and kicked this way and that!

Christ it stunk. You don't realize what water does to tame the reek until some homeless maggot shits on the floor in front of you.

"So I'm like, 'Look pal, do you mind!'

And he comes back in between grunts, 'No, I don't mind! Smell the love!'

"Christ can you imagine how bad it's going to be this winter with this dirt bag doing his shit bombings?

"You would think he'd have some self-respect—at least wash his hands. But no, he pulls up his pants, shit dangling from the cuff and smeared along the floor, walks up to the sink, and doesn't even wash his hands, just admires himself in the mirror. That's when I saw him—that little dirt bag."

I value this Denizen Kane sighting at highly probable, and will stake my cryptoghettology degree on it. And if it wasn't him, it's either an understudy or a rival.

A Harm City Evening: A Change-of-season Threat Assessment

© 2014 James LaFond

Yesterday afternoon I made me seasonal scout. When the weather changes behaviors change. As I am on foot in this habitat, whenever the change of seasons come I devote an evening to just poking around, acquainting myself with new characters and indications of possible new patterns, reacquainting myself with the perennial crimescape.

The Freaks and Corner Boys

A teenager in winter attire, boots, slacks, hoody, and fitted had, with underwear matching his brown slacks and his left hand down his pants holding his identity, passed me on the sidewalk. A petite couple in their mid twenties, he with a full beard and a tri-colored tattooed neck and guitar, and her with multiple facial piercings, were scrounging used cigarettes from the gutter. I crossed the street and passed a crowd of younger teenagers horse playing and hanging out. A hunched crack whore ducked through the shrubbery and went on her way from the direction of the crack house up the side street to my right.

Across the street to my left at the service station five boys about 16 hung out in their summer attire: sneakers, cargo shorts, double T-shirts and fitted hats. The smallest boy kept an eye on me and did not let e out of his sight. Last year these boys waited on this side of the street and followed middle aged men into the neighborhoods and bum rushed them while car mounted adults staked out the service station. The car mounted muggers have been absent for a year now and these guys have scaled back the violence and seemed to be concentrating on the drug trade and young ladies, one of whom they are admiring as I pass.

The White Vice Lords

A handicapped boy is panhandling on the corner under the protection of the White Vice Lords, one of whom is patrolling the area, looking like Eminem on steroids with his fitted hat and windbreaker. I run into Hawk at the grocer and he asks me to stop into the bar later so he can buy me a drink and we can talk boxing.

I Head back through the alley and back lots and spot two younger boys, one 8 one 13, waiting for somebody. As I walk the side street behind the service station a big bearded skin head pulls out of a driveway in a pickup truck and does not bother threatening me. I must truly be getting old.

The County Run

I bussed it out to the county to shop for my grandson's birthday party. The bus traffic is light and I am alone on a bus stop when a really cute blonde cop in her late 20s questions me about a gold van that was seen abducting a little girl in Essex.

Mrs. Morrison

Coming back into town just after darkness falls I run into Mrs. Morrison at the bar. She said she had a story for me so I decided to get us a cheese pizza down on the corner.

Upon my return the three women in the front of the bar started chanting "FAK, FAK, FAK!" as they pointed at me and laughed.

In answer to my questioning look the chick from New York said, 'How are you going to eat that pizza without your fork and knife mister high class writer? We're not going to call you Secret Window anymore. You're ForkAndKnife now—FAK, FAK."

I mustered what dignity I might. "I was not going to suffer your ridicule again for eating like a civilized person, so have brought no flatware to your den of squalor."

Her partner in character assassination chimed in, "Are you sure you're going to be able to handle that pizza without a knife and fork hon?"

"Oh, I have seen you barbarians conducting your uncouth feast often. I shall simply ape you."

"Oooooo!" they heckled and left me to my interview.

Mrs. Morrison begins telling me about her adventure at the news stand.

"I walked by this thirty year old black guy and he says, 'Hi.'

"I say, 'Hi' and keep on walking.

He gets in front of me and says, "Do you want a boy friend?"

"I said, 'No!' and keep walking.

"He follows me inside and says, 'Do you have a boy friend?'

"I said, 'No, I have a husband!'

"He said, 'I live right around the corner. After working all day don't you want to put your feet up?'

"I said, 'No! I'm fifty-five years old.'

"He won't let up and says, 'Do you have a daughter?' How do you even answer that? What a loser. So I just ignore him.

"He goes on, 'Oh I heard you work up at the bar, en you like us black guys, give us a break on our drinks.'

[Points at buxom bar maid and then motions to her own slight form] "I don't have a set of giant boobs! Get lost pal! Scram, later!" and the entire time his hand is in his pants playing with his thing. I get customers at the dealership, men, grown men in their forties and fifties, hands in their pants playing with their thing. What is up with these black men? Could you tell me? Do you know why they are constantly playing with themselves in public?"

"They are holding on to their identity, their social worth, what there is of it. The women just use them as breeding drones to get welfare. They live off the food and money intended for the children. We see it in supermarkets all the time."

The black off duty police detective sitting on my other side chimes in. "You know that's right. I know a woman who is making forty-eight-thousand dollars a year on getting knocked up. She has a boyfriend who is not father to any of those three men that knocked her up. She has a child by a fireman, a child by a UPS man, and a child by a police! Forty-eight grand a year to spreads your legs and drop an egg!

"And now, and now I got to deal with those muthafucas that these bitches be hatchin'. I'm sittin' across from this muthafuca at my desk today en he eyeballing me—eye-fucking me!"

Hawk has taken a seat at the bar and has sent me over a hard cider and fireball cocktail.

The irate detective continues, "Don't you know I almost went over the desk after him. He is sitting there telling me, 'Its commin',' and making like this [shows gangbanger pistol grip]. I told my supervisor, 'This piece of shit is not even an adult and he is threatening my life, telling me he knows who I am and its coming!"

Mrs. Morrison, her story over, was socializing with her lady friends. The detective was now arguing with someone on the phone, and Hawk was itching to talk about the latest Floyd Money fight.

Violence against middle-aged male pedestrians in Hamilton is at about half the level it was last year and into the early summer. There is no greater police presence. In fact, other than drug busts and domestics there is little police action apparent around here.

I do not know what the reason is, but am happy to have been taken off of the top slot on the menu.

Zombie Bait #1: When the Zombies Rise Stake These Two Out First

© 2014 James LaFond

Anthropologist Lionel Tiger has recently coined the term 'Bureaugamy' to describe the rising kinship system that dominates American urban life. The three components of this 'family' are a woman, a baby, and a government official. Men only relate to this system as breeding drones and entertainers. When not providing one of these services they are generally intoxicated or incarcerated. Last night on the bus I was ringside for this sniveling new world.

If the Zombie Apocalypse had been underway at 10:30 p.m. last night I would have tossed the following two human devolution experiments out the back door to the walkers.

A mixed race teenage girl with dyed red hair boarded the bus with her BFF [a white girl with smartphone], her semi-employed drone [a skinny black kid with an afro] charged with piloting the baby stroller, and a little brown baby of perhaps 11 months.

What time was this again?

The baby, tired of being dragged around to fast food joints and T-mobile outlets on a wintry night, began to cry as the mother sat him on her lap next to me. Mom wiped her runny nose on the sleeve of her new coat, slapped the baby in the back of the head, and said, "Shut up before I bang you in your mouth!"

Thank you miss, if I'm still around in 16 years when this brutalized product of your neglect is walking the streets looking for old white dudes to bank, I'll surely be too old to outrun him.

Feed her to the zekes!

A few minutes later an unemployed drone, drunk out of his mind, stepped up unto the bus and refused to put his money in the meter until he had said his piece about the Superbowl. The bus driver asked him to pay and he got louder and held the bus up for another five minutes. The bus driver then asked him to get off and the drunk became threatening and—since he is white and obviously trying to get me dragged into a race riot—began making racial slurs.

Eventually he called the driver—who is a friend of mine—an asshole, and strode to the back of the bus with his half drunk forty of Bud Light—the universally renowned beverage of jerks.

I continued reading my book, but, but! If we had a zombie apocalypse going on I would have hamstrung him with my razor, knocked his remaining two teeth out with my steel toes, and tossed him to the zekes!

Have a nice day, support your local bureaugamist, and throw that panhandler under the wheels of this bus, please.

Zombie Bait #2: 10 Arguments For White Genocide

For those street geeks, losers, freaks, and assorted dysgenic bi-products of our sick society who do not make the Panhandler Nation or Streets Have Eyes grade [Yes, we have standards here.] I have, in an all-inclusive, liberal, group-hug kind of way, consented to give them equal time with such legends as Stick, Decker, Denizen Kane and T-Bone. Being zombie bait, designated as terrestrial chum in the all-too-likely event of a Zombie Apocalypse, may not seem like much.

What can I say pal, its free.

The Dumbest Whiteman in Baltimore

This idiot spent 45 minutes this morning complaining to and threatening the female bus driver, because of the before school traffic that she had less than no influence over. As the blacks began laughing at him I cringed in embarrassment—since I look white, and might have been mistaken for a distant relative of his. Then seeing that he had an audience he picked on this skinny teenage girl who was scared to death of him, wooing her with race-mixing sexual innuendo, and even getting on his federal cell phone and telling an imaginary friend that he was bringing a 'Puerto Rican girl' with him. He did redeem himself somewhat in my eyes when he called for the death of the Maryland Plantation Master, Governor O'Mick.

Here is a direct quote, as I sat six inches from him writing while he spewed, "Let me run the fuckin' show! You Ain't worth a shit! Let me fuckin' drive! Da gobment ain't worth a shit. I should be in charge! Get me some Puerto Rican girls—ain't about color—it 'bout who you is! I ain't stupid. I got a piss too! We ain't goin' no where. I should have kept my dumbass home."

I agree.

I know this job slacking piece-of-filth from the time he tried to buy some oxys from me, thinking that any decent white dude has to be a junkie like him. He is 51 years old, which makes him possibly the oldest whigger in the world. He dresses like

Eminem and talks with the ebonic gangster finger spread. Of course, even though he is threatening women and saying the f-word every other sentence, we can't put our hands on him because of the new security camera system. At first I liked the security cameras, but now it has done nothing but enabled rudeness and threats, leaving the cretins like this fool safe from harm lest the goons of the Mommy Sate descend upon us for cleaning up another one of nature's mistakes.

Ah, for the Zombie Apocalypse. I would dropkick him from the back door to the swarming zekes!

Fat, White & Affluent in Maryland

Last night, at 12:01 foodstamps broke! By 12:23 we had families of fat people pushing their duos of overflowing shopping carts to the checkout at Ghetto Grocer Getaway.

First came the three white trashian drug addicts, drooling on the belt, dropping half-eaten doughnuts, and cussing as they reached for things that were not there—"Where'd it go man!"

A $200+ order with over $500 left in their account.

Next came the 20-year-old breeder with her 9-year-old son, who she was cursing at and slapping and threatening to 'beat'. She rang out over $300 and sent him back in for more.

Finally came a tall bald, fat man with expensive hip-hop attire, a gigantic son sporting the same, and two breeders, dolled up with designer purses and hair extensions. All of these smiling, snack and soda and steak purchasing cretins had plenty of expensive ink on their arms. They spent $340 and change, and left in an SUV with over $400 remaining on their card.

If the zombie apocalypse comes I suggest we stake these fat buckets of degenerate DNA at busy intersections. The zekes should be able to feed extensively on these while we cross the street down the road a ways.

I realize, that if you don't know me, that you might think I am joking with this Zombie Bait series. I will not hold that against you—it's kind of quaint.

Merely Reprehensible: Zombie Bait #3

This morning, out in Harm County, where the white buffalo roam in their Dodge Ram 4-by-4's, I was finishing up the frozen food case for Mister John, at Free Food For Fat F...s, when **he** entered'; a man with no name; a man worthy of no name; a sign of the times; a tic on the body politic.

I know that all of you liberals assume he is a handicapped ghetto kid, who, if you put Johnny Knoxville in charge of testing at an Ivy League school, might be able to gain admittance.

Of course you conservatives think he is a milk-sucking stay-at-home liberal dad.

Yes, and you MANLY 'manosphere' MEN are certain that he must be a she, or at least a he-she, at best a feminist.

You libertarians are certain that he is a government employee, like all of the cops that pay for their groceries with food stamps in Baltimore.

And you alternative right guys—and you, you loan alternative right babe—are certain that he is an illegal alien; probably some godforsaken 'mud-person' from south of the border, come here to take from you what your great, great, great, great worked-to-death grand daddy's master took from some Stone Age holdover with a feather in his hair and a tear rolling over his cheek...

But really, who is this man with no name, this Clint Eastwood of State subsidized groceries?

The answer is: he is merely reprehensible. I began the Zombie Bait series so that those purely parasitical proto-hominid effluvia deposits on the body economic would not be elevated to the level of such Streets Have Eyes characters as Denizen Cane, Bruce the Bricklayer, Newnetthelove, Jervis the Cabbie, and other Harm City legends. This male of the Homo Foodstamponid branch of our devolutionary tree, is—merely reprehensible!

Just after 6:00 this morning, Merely Reprehensible strolled in as Angie—who is retired, but can't make her gas & electric payment, so has to work the FFFFF register for the morning breakfast crowd stopping in for their bagels, doughnuts and yogurt on their way to work—logged onto her cash register.

He is a middle-aged white man who owns a small construction company and employs a mangy thirty-something drowned rat of a helper, who stood by nervously as they shopped and then cut into line with a full basket of meat and ice cream just ahead of a coffee and doughnut order. By the time his $218 worth of steaks and nutty buddy bars were rung up, there were three additional single item customers stuck in line behind him.

Then, as the order was totaled, and Angie said, "Enter your pin number Sir", the order was denied, as he had entered the wrong pin number. This was retried numerous times. We now had six customers in line. Angie then paged the manager, who paged the courtesy babe, who called Merely Reprehensible over to the window so that he could call up the junkie that had sold him an EBT card with $220 on it for $100 dollars.

We were now eight working stiffs deep at the register as our NFL representative [he was wearing

Baltimore Ravens attire] kept questioning the junkie on the other end of the land line as to the correct pin number. We can only presume that the junkie knew his baby's mama's pin number. However, he had apparently injected sufficient liquid assets into his bioconomy to render him Simply Incomprehensible.

The man and his helper said they would be 'right back', and left the store. Angie rang out her customers, placed the nutty buddys in the freezer, rolled the meat into the meat room, and saved the receipt. By 8:00 she was swamped by legit customers. By 9:00, when I left, the nutty buddys were looking right lonely.

Okay, let's say next month, when Merely Reprehensible and his emaciated helper show up to commit food stamp fraud, the Zombie Apocalypse hits. What will my last act as an FFFFF clerk be before the Zekes overrun the store?

I will grab a 24 ounce longneck glass bottle of Everfresh mango-carrot flavored juice beverage, and use it to brain the emaciated helper. I will then kick his employer in the balls with my steel toe boot. Then, as I tell the FFFFF employees and customers to flee out the back door behind produce, I will deploy my trusty case cutter, eviscerate the helper, and use his entrails to tie his employer down on Angie's now pretty funky register—sorry Angie.

In this way, as we make our way out the back and leap off of the produce dock, we will know that the Zekes are coming as soon as Merely Reprehensible ceases his I'm-being-eaten-alive-and-this-is-not-cable-TV-and-therefore-really-sucks howls of anguish.

You know, I thought Jack Donovan was nuts when he evoked the 'zombie apocalypse' as a solution to liberal feminism. But you know what Jack: I think I'm stoked for this thing. There is more than enough zombie bait to go around in this town.

Disclaimer

No zombies were abused, injured or mistreated in the composition of this work.

'Dreadlocked': Zombie Bait #4

© 2014 James LaFond

This morning, 5/1/14, at 2:49 AM, just after those Wednesday night drunks had been carted home by Harm County cabbies, or had stumbled into a ditch all on their own, or had been compassionately aided in their quest for a place to lay their head by a Harm County peace office, Swick, a local cabbie, came through the front door to purchase his day's groceries. He is a large light-skinned man who stands about six four, sports a chromed dome, and leans wearily on his shopping cart.

I sit by the door at the bench reading a horror story by Richard Matheson. Swick is up front within a page and a half and Bubba, who mans the FFFFF register, asks, "So how has your night been?"

Swick's face tightens up. Then his cheeks relax as he spies me, a chronologically sympathetic soul, and begins to drawl in a Carolina accent, "Almost got in a fight: a young boy, perhaps twenny-five. I've picked him up before, en knew he wasn't goin' far, so wanted to cut him a break. I flip off the meter [which calculates over $2 for just getting in]. After all he jus' goin' roun' the way from here, en I need to shop. So I say, 'How much you lookin' ta spend?'

"He says, all indignant, 'What? You messin' wit me—wit me! Triflin' wit ma shit!'

"Now, I jus tryin' to cut him a break on the fare. I've had my nut since ten. Then he gets out and slams my cab door en says, 'I could take this shit if I wanted. This bitch could be mine—I could take it!'

"You might be but twenny-five—but a buck-sixty en talkin' dat shit about my ride—you need ta back that up! I got out, slammed the door, lean ova the hood, 'Boy, I will wrap dem stinky-ass dreadlocks around your neck and drag you down the road!'

"He didn' stop runnin' his mouth, but he didn' stop walkin' eitha. Second time this week a young boy threaten me for no reason, jus' to lay the threat. I can only take but so much a that. Strangle him with 'is own nasty-ass hair I say. You have a nice day sir."

Now, come the Zombie Apocalypse, staking this dreadlocked miscreant out for the zekes will be made easier by the funky carry straps on his head.

Also, since he is a proven vocalizer, we want his cries of anguish to draw as many zekes off our trail as possible. So let's take off his shoes so they can start eating him from the feet up, rather than head first.

That might sound heartless Bro. But when the diseased brains hit the fan every second counts!

Midnight at the Zombie Apocalypse: A 'Please Dad' Coat Zombie Bait Adventure

© 2014 James LaFond

On Friday night it was raining and I did not want to throw the duster on that I had worn to the overcast funeral at which I served as a pallbearer earlier in the day. I armed myself against the rain with pointy wooden umbrella and the 'Please Dad' coat, which is the 40 year old canvas bomber jacket which elicits a groan from my youngest son when I wear it out to dinner, even when going to the diner. He'll shake his head as I get in his car that cost more than the house we raised him in and groan, 'Please Dad, I want to eat something better than pizza tonight and you look like a homeless guy."

In a sane rainy world at midnight the 'Please Dad' coat would serve me as a protection from panhandling talisman. But it was not to be. As I arrived at the front walk of Free Food For Fat F...s having missed the half hour clock-in slot by 2 minutes, I decided to speak with a collaborator about a project on my 9 year old shell phone with no back for a few moments more until 11:45.

It was not to be. I had somehow walked through a dimension door into a world where I occupied the top economic rung on the societal ladder!

Two zombies and a zombie caller were on site. I was beseeched by the zombie caller who was dressed at $20K a year better than I, and who had a nice knew car, and spoke very loud and haltingly— in the oratory style of the impatient drug-damaged brain.

"Hey man! Can you spare a dollar?"

I shook my head 'no'.

Not perceiving subtle body language through the echoing haze that was the scorched wasteland of his sensory array, he amped it up, "Excuse me! Any fuckin' help here? I need a dollar!"

I eye-fucked him and snarled and he backed off. He then looked off my left shoulder and said, to the horrific image of a voodoo zombie wearing nothing but a sheet, "Hello, a dollar maybe?"

This fool was asking a black as night being so brain dead as to be floating in a trance—eyes wide shut—wrapped in a dirty bed sheet against the rain and sipping absently from a partially drunk cup of cold coffee, for a dollar. The voodoo zombie next to me seemed a creature not only entirely destitute, but of pre-monetary origin. What ass would beg from a person in seemingly third-world quality squalor?

"Who panhandles that?" I thought. This dude is an actual zombie and could be one of Jeanott's minions from my horror writing.

The zombie caller threw up his hands as if he was looking at two idiots that don't speak his language—and I suppose he was, and marched indignantly into the store. I find out later that he was spending food stamps and needed a dollar to cover a nonfood item—chap stick I think.

Note: By my humble calculations 25% of all welfare payments, including food stamps, are utilized first to purchase illegal drugs, before they are converted back into the other economy, which may not forever be the mainstream one.

Then, as the Haitian zombie floated by me in his sheet and I closed out my call an African American zombie approached me. He had been standing off out in the pouring rain, hands in the pockets of his drenched windbreaker, staring vacantly at me as if he thought I might be John the Baptist but was not sure if this gutter was the river Jordon. He looked at me in hopefully stunned dread, like a space walker who thinks his tether might have detached from its anchor and is about to plunge into the hostile atmosphere of the planet below.

He stayed there in the dark rain. Latter he will approach me inside and mumble something to me, then apologize, step outside, and hurl white vomit all over the parcel pickup area. Hmm, a penitent vomiting zombie—that is a twist.

Now, in case of the Zombie Apocalypse, I suggest encouraging the Haitian zombies and any penitent hurling zombies to accompany us as flankers. On the other hand, if a zombie caller shows up and begins loudly making demands in his deadzone drone, stake him out for the zekes! His 'Hey man!' call will carry through the post apocalyptic night to draw the zekes off of our trail.

In any potential survival scenario, whether a natural or unnatural disaster, I could not imagine coexisting with the zombie caller for more than the time it takes to convert him into a tool or resource.

Harm City Devolution: 3 Handicapped Douche Bags versus a Spunky Pizza Dispatcher in a Zombie Bait Mugging

© 2014 James LaFond

I was headed down into the hood on Sunday afternoon. The streets were barren as the football game was on. This is when terrorists will take over American cities, while the local football team is playing.

From a distance I noticed three local characters: two unnamed deaf guys in their 30s, one white one black, and a giant idiot some call 'Lurch'. Lurch makes no attempt to communicate with these other two, just follows them zombie like.

Down the street, a hundred yards to my left, Celine, the dispatcher at the pizzeria, is walking to work, her purse tucked under her arm, eying the trio across the street with some concern.

Lurch is pretty much attached to Deaf Brown. Deaf Brown is communicating with Deaf Pale, not in real sign language, but in made up signs, points, grunts and foot jittering pantomime one would think worthy of Homo Jerkoffacus, back in the dim prehistory of Harm City. It is obvious from my distance that Deaf Pale is indicating that Deaf Brown and Lurch must go get Celine—'intercept that bitch, for she is nearly to her destination—the pizzeria!'

Deaf Brown and Lurch shuffle over to the left hand side of the road and take up a blocking position 50 yards before Celine, who reads this move and darts through the sparse traffic to gain the side walk on Deaf Pale's side of the street, whereupon she stops, turns, and gives the finger to her incompetent pursuers.

Deaf Pale jumps up and down like an angry chimp and waves at Deaf Brown and Lurch who seem confused, and who fail to comprehend his further instructions at this distance.

I crossed the street diagonally from left to right, causing Deaf Brown and Lurch to disperse and mill aimlessly, while Deaf Pale shook his fists at the ground—known by idiots the world over to be guilty of foiling many a well-laid plan—and headed up to the crack house where he hangs out.

I followed Celine to work and asked her what was up. "Oh that scrawny fucker is mad at me for not giving him free food and not giving him cash for something he said he found and that belonged to one of our customers. I put it in lost and found and he hit the roof when I told him to get lost. Mute maybe, but deaf he is not."

I gave Celine a lesson in stabbing with her order-taking ink pen, admonished her not to take on all three of her stalkers at once, and told her to tell her boss. Unfortunately, any man in her life who might want to discourage or punish this witlessly ill-intentioned trio would run the risk of offending the Momyocracy that rules guilt-ridden America and is only capable of seeing these two deaf creeps and their retarded muscle as victims.

I know this is a Zombie Bait article, and one might expect me to cry for Deaf Pale, Deaf Brown and Lurch to be staked out for the zekes—but they are the zekes! The zombies are here, right where the corporate white guilt mommy nation effete want them to be.

Note: If you have been struck with the thought that police should have been there to make the streets safe for Celine, then you are not living on the same planet where your mind does reside, and a prudent survivor of a zombie apocalypse might opt to stake you out for the zekes! as you babble on about calling the police. Police are not, and never have been intended by our masters, to be the agents or guardians of our safety. That is a Hollywood fantasy. Celine lives and works in the real world, where the police are watching the game like the rest of the loyal citizens of a morally handicapped douche bag-ruled nation of proto-zombies.